Learn FRENCH Through Fairy Tales

Cinderella

Book Design & Production: Slangman Kids *(a division of Slangman Inc. and Slangman Publishing)*

Copy Editor: Julie Bobrick
Illustrated by: "Migs!" Sandoval
Translator: "Slangman" David Burke
Proofreader: Emmanuelle Rousseaux

Published by: Slangman Kids *(a division of Slangman Inc. and Slangman Publishing)* 12206 Hillslope Street, Studio City, CA 91604 •USA • Toll Free Telephone from USA: 1-877-SLANGMAN (1-877-752-6462) • From outside the USA: 1-818-SLANGMAN (1-818-752-6462) • Worldwide Fax 1-413-647-1589 • Email: info@slangman.com • Website: www.slangman.com

"Migs!" Sandoval ✳ our illustrator ✳

Miguel *"Migs!"* Sandoval has been drawing cartoons since the age of 6 and has worked on numerous national commercials and movies as a sculptor, model builder, and illustrator. He was born in Los Angeles and was raised in a bilingual household, speaking English and Spanish. He currently lives in San Francisco where he is working on his new comic book series!

ISBN10: 1891888-757
ISBN13: 978189888-755
Printed in the U.S.A.

10 9 8 7 6 5 4 3 2 1

Order Form

Preview chapters & shop online!
www.slangman.com

SHIP TO: _____

_____

_____

_____

Contact/Phone/Email: _____

SHIPPING

Domestic Orders
SURFACE MAIL
(Delivery time 5-7 business days).
Add $5 shipping/handling for the first item, $1.50 for each additional item.

RUSH SERVICE
Available at extra charge. Contact us for details.

International Orders
SURFACE MAIL
(Delivery time 6-8 weeks).
Add $6 shipping/handling for the first item, $2 for each additional item. Note that shipping to some countries may be more expensive. Contact us for details.

AIRMAIL (approx. 3-5 business days)
Available at extra charge. Contact us for details.

Method of Payment (Check one):

☐ Personal Check or Money Order
   (Must be in U.S. funds and drawn on a U.S. bank.)

☐ VISA ☐ Master Card ☐ Discover ☐ American Express ☐ JCB

Credit Card Number

Signature _____   Expiration Date ☐☐ ☐☐

QTY	ISBN-13	TITLE	PRICE	LEVEL	TOTAL COST
English to CHINESE (Mandarin)					
	9781891888-793	Cinderella	$14.95	1	
	9781891888-854	Goldilocks	$14.95	2	
	9781891888-915	Beauty and the Beast	$14.95	3	
English to FRENCH					
	9781891888-755	Cinderella	$14.95	1	
	9781891888-816	Goldilocks	$14.95	2	
	9781891888-878	Beauty and the Beast	$14.95	3	
English to GERMAN					
	9781891888-762	Cinderella	$14.95	1	
	9781891888-830	Goldilocks	$14.95	2	
	9781891888-885	Beauty and the Beast	$14.95	3	
English to HEBREW					
	9781891888-922	Cinderella	$14.95	1	
	9781891888-939	Goldilocks	$14.95	2	
	9781891888-946	Beauty and the Beast	$14.95	3	
English to ITALIAN					
	9781891888-779	Cinderella	$14.95	1	
	9781891888-823	Goldilocks	$14.95	2	
	9781891888-892	Beauty and the Beast	$14.95	3	
English to JAPANESE					
	9781891888-786	Cinderella	$14.95	1	
	9781891888-847	Goldilocks	$14.95	2	
	9781891888-908	Beauty and the Beast	$14.95	3	
English to SPANISH					
	9781891888-748	Cinderella	$14.95	1	
	9781891888-809	Goldilocks	$14.95	2	
	9781891888-861	Beauty and the Beast	$14.95	3	
Japanese to ENGLISH 絵本で えいご を学ぼう					
	9781891888-038	Cinderella	$14.95	1	
	9781891888-045	Goldilocks	$14.95	2	
	9781891888-052	Beauty and the Beast	$14.95	3	
Korean to ENGLISH 동화를 통한 ENGLISH 배우기					
	9781891888-076	Cinderella	$14.95	1	
	9781891888-106	Goldilocks	$14.95	2	
	9781891888-113	Beauty and the Beast	$14.95	3	
Spanish to ENGLISH Aprende INGLÉS con cuentos de hadas					
	9781891888-953	Cinderella	$14.95	1	
	9781891888-960	Goldilocks	$14.95	2	
	9781891888-977	Beauty and the Beast	$14.95	3	

Total for Merchandise _____

Sales Tax *(California residents only add applicable sales tax)* _____

Shipping *(See left)* _____

ORDER GRAND TOTAL _____

Prices subject to change

SLANGMAN® KIDS
(a division of Slangman Publishing)

** TO PLACE AN ORDER - CALL, FAX, OR EMAIL: **
Phone: 1-818-752-6462 • Fax: 1-413-647-1589
Email: info@slangman.com • Web: www.slangman.com
12206 Hillslope Street • Studio City, CA 91604

(FORM 071606)

Dedication

The entire "Foreign Language Through Fairy Tales" series is dedicated to all the children of the world.

It is through their understanding, appreciation, and celebration of our differences that the world will become a better and safer place for us all.

1

fille ←

belle ←

maison ←

Once upon a time, there lived a (girl) named Cinderella who was very (pretty). The **belle fille** lived in a small (house) with her stepmother and

two stepsisters. At times it was difficult for the **belle fille** to live in such a small **maison** with her stepmother and two stepsisters. Why? Because they were

3

méchante ← jealous that she was so **belle** which is why her stepmother was extra [mean] to her. But the **belle fille** never complained about living in a small

maison with her **méchante** stepmother and two stepsisters, even though
they forced her to do all the work in the
entire **maison** day in and day out!

5

Royal Invitation

Who: The King

What: A Royal Ball

Where: The Castle

When: This Saturday, 8pm

Why: To find a wife for the prince

Valet parking available

One day, a royal invitation arrived at the **maison** of the **belle fille**. The king was throwing a [party] for the prince. And the **fête** was going to be [big].

fête ←

grande ←

A **grande fête**! The prince was very handsome and it was at this **grande fête** that the **beau** prince hoped to find the **belle** wife he had been seeking.

→ **beau**

→ **épouse**

7

prince

The king and queen also hoped the **beau prince** would find a **belle épouse** at the **grande fête** because they wanted their son, the **beau prince**, to be happy.

8

The night of the **grande fête** for the **beau prince** arrived but Cinderella was sad because her **méchante** stepmother wouldn't let her leave the **maison**!

triste

9

Poor, **triste** Cinderella had to stay in her **maison** and never get the chance to meet the **beau prince** at the **grande fête** and become his **épouse**.

Then she heard a voice say, "My dear, I'm your fairy godmother and you'll be able to go to the **grande fête** and you'll be wearing a **belle** dress!"

robe

11

And with a wave of her wand, Cinderella was now wearing a **belle robe** made of the finest silk. "Oh, thank you! **Merci**!" exclaimed Cinderella. She was

merci

a **belle fille** wearing a **belle robe**,
and eager to leave her **maison** to meet
the **beau prince** at the **grande fête**
in hopes of becoming his **épouse**!

moment ←

minuit ←

"One moment!" the fairy godmother added. "Make sure to leave the **grande fête** by midnight because your **belle robe** will change back to what it was!"

Cinderella thought for a **moment** then said, "I'll remember to leave before **minuit**." And with that, the **belle fille** left for the **grande fête**. She was

15

heureuse ←

no longer **triste**, but very (happy) to be meeting the **beau prince**. As she got out of her carriage, she could hear the **grande fête**! Cinderella walked in

and wasn't too **heureuse** to see more
than one **belle fille** waiting to meet the
beau prince. But after a **moment**,
she calmed down and was ready to

17

meet the **beau prince** face to face. And
beau he was! She could hardly believe
her eyes! And it was clear the **beau
prince** was in love with the **belle**

amoureux

18

fille the very first **moment** he saw her!
"**Merci** for inviting me" said Cinderella.
"You're welcome" responded the
beau prince. They danced and

De rien

danced for hours, until the stroke of **minuit** was upon them which the **belle fille** had completely forgotten about! Poof! Her **belle robe** vanished!

20

Au revoir

"Goodbye!" shouted Cinderella.

"**Au revoir** and **merci** for inviting me!"

"**De rien**," responded the **beau prince**.

And Cinderella ran back to her **maison**.

21

chaussure ←

The only thing she left behind was a glass shoe. The **beau prince** was extremely **triste** and went from town to town looking for a **belle fille** whose

22

pied

[foot] would fit the glass **chaussure**.
After days of eliminating **belle fille**
after **belle fille**, the **beau prince**
was even more **triste** than ever, but he

had one more **maison** to visit. The **méchante** stepmother and two stepsisters ran out to try on the glass **chaussure**, but it was no use. He still couldn't find a **pied** to match the **chaussure**.

The **beau prince** was **triste** and about to give up, but at that very **moment**, he spotted Cinderella. There was something special about her.

He just had to see if her **pied** was the one that could fit the glass **chaussure**. He knelt down in front of her and slid the **chaussure** on her **pied**.

And her **pied** fit the glass **chaussure**
perfectly! At that very **moment**,
Cinderella's fairy godmother reappeared
and changed her back into the same

belle fille in the **belle robe** the **beau prince** had met at his **grande fête**. He was now more **amoureux** than ever! The **belle fille** was **heureuse**

that she lost her glass **chaussure** at the **grande fête** or the **beau prince** may never have found her! Soon, Cinderella became his **épouse**. She was so very

heureuse! She would never, ever be **triste** again. And the **beau prince** and the **belle fille**, Cinderella, lived in the castle happily ever after.